C000240717

DOTTIE'S DIARY

❧

THE CURIOUS INCIDENT
OF A
ROYAL BULL TERRIER

❧

BY
EMMA SERGEANT

HarperCollins*Publishers*

HarperCollins*Entertainment*
An Imprint of HarperCollins*Publishers*
77–85 Fulham Palace Road,
Hammersmith, London W6 8JB
www.harpercollins.co.uk

Published by HarperCollinsEntertainment 2004
1 3 5 7 9 8 6 4 2
Copyright © Emma Sergeant 2004

The Author asserts the moral right
to be identified as the author of this work

A catalogue record for this book is available from the British Library
ISBN 0 00 7197470

Set in Centaur
Printed and bound by Proost NV, Turnhout, Belgium

All rights reserved. No part of this publication may be reproduced,
stored in a retrieval system, or transmitted, in any form or by any means,
electronic, mechanical, photocopying, recording or otherwise,
without the prior permission of the publishers.

THE KENNEL CLUB

Registration Certificate for: IMPERIAL ARIELLA   MO2   Registration No.   M2944104MO2

Breed BULL TERRIER   Sex BITCH   Born 21/05/87 Registered   10/06/87

Colour BRINDLE & WHITE   Breeder MR & MRS F G ENGLISH

Sire MAXIMILLIAN BULLY BOY OF JOBRULU   CH   FO4   4720BR

Dam CULRATHAN MISTRESS EM   KO9   K3636704KO9

Owned by   MR & MRS F G ENGLISH
                  70 SHUTTLEWORTH ROAD
                  BATTERSEA
                  LONDON SW11 3DF

                                                                                    02/06/87 10/06/87

The issue of this certificate does not guarantee its accuracy as it is based on details supplied to The Kennel Club by the applicant. The code which follows
the name of a dog indicates the month and year of the issue of the KCSB Breed Records Supplement in which the notice of the registration appears.

Wake up at 6.35 am, five minutes before the cook arrives.

Florence is still asleep. She must be feeling rough after scoffing all those chocolate liqueurs. Serves her right for doing a solo raid.

Even my stretch, shake and wind routine fails to rouse the drunken Florence.

I wait for the cook to start frying the bacon. I position myself behind her solid calves and lurk in the hope that she will step back, trip and tip the frying pan's contents into my gentle, smiling jaws. Until now nothing is left in reach and she handles the fly swatter in a truly menacing way. She merits respect because she is the conduit of bones and dinner.

DOTTIE AND HER COEVALS — THEY SHARE BIRTHDAYS, BONES AND BAD DEEDS.

Mummy enters the breakfast room at 7.30 am. Lots of pats. Sometimes I fail to tell the difference between a pat and a smack. Both seem to make her feel better. I love Mummy. She is a sporty, brave lady and refreshingly direct.

Mummy starts breakfast. I place my front paw on her foot and lean heavily. I like to keep the pressure on when food is about.

Florence wanders in looking grim and collapses under the breakfast table. The chocolate liqueurs must be on the move. She produces a superlative sample from her arsenal of lethal gasses and clears the breakfast room of human life.

MY IDEA OF ANGER MANAGEMENT IS WHEN ROOM SERVICE IS LATE. ▶

I leap on Mummy's chair and lick clean her abandoned plate. Her diary is open and I see that tomorrow we are off to Mummy's Mummy for Christmas, which means I will see Melchior.

Besides greed, my other fixation is my lust for Melchior. He is a black Labrador. His Daddy is my Mummy's elder brother. I wait all year for a brief sighting of this masterpiece of masculinity.

I leave the breakfast room satisfied. Florence heads off for a long session in the garden. I will tell her the good news later.

I love Mummy

Meanwhile, where is Eglantine? I find her (the last of our sisterhood) in the boot room. Eglantine thinks there is a possibility of a walk and is trying to do unspeakably passionate things to Mummy's left leg.

We are only going to the stables. Walks in public places are off the schedule after my bad behaviour in the park. By the time I understood that the soft, yielding flesh in my mouth was a child and not an intruder it was too late. After the third wallop from Mummy I realised that it was not a pat but a more savage communication.

MUMMY MUST TRY HARDER.

By this time Florence and Eglantine were trying to be supportive. This seemed to further agitate the child, still firmly held in my mouth. Judging from the sporting looks on Florence and Eglantine's faces, the child was safer with me.

How can you say sorry with your mouth full? I feel misunderstood. Mauling children has never been a pastime of mine. It is just unfortunate if they are holding objects of mutual interest like balls or biscuits.

OCCASIONALLY I CAN ENTERTAIN MYSELF.

I always enjoy a visit to the stables, although I do not understand Mummy's affection for horses. Why does she want to murmur sweet nothings to those unpredictable monsters with lips like marshmallows? Eglantine, Florence and I have discussed it and feel Mummy must be saved from her unnatural passion for these flighty monsters. This involves different strategies.

Today I will try sitting outside the stable door and wait for Mummy's chestnut mare to lower her head. One of the evolutionary joys of bull terriers, and duck-billed platypuses for that matter, is that our eyes are on top of our cranium. This can be annoying when it rains but an advantage when it comes to overhead observation.

I AM A PEDIGREE BITCH BUT I ALLOW THE LESS WELL-BORN TO APPROACH SOMETIMES. ▶

I am a pedigree
bitch
but I allow
the less

well born
to approach

sometimes

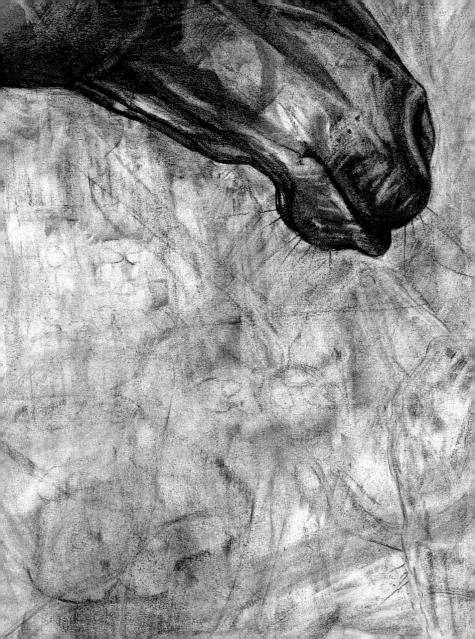

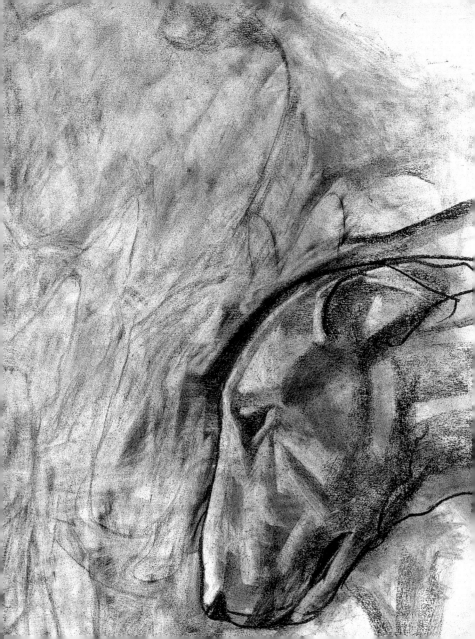

The chestnut's marshmallow lips come into range, I leap and snap. Unfortunately, I miss. The surprised horse hits her head, which is some comfort but still not first prize.

What next? I do love the stables, as there is always something to pursue or chew or both. Mummy found the chestnut quite tranquil. Clearly half-concussing the monster worked a treat.

The rest of the day is spent watching the packing and Mummy checking the Christmas presents. Every preparation is a joyous step nearer to Melchior – oh, ephemeral epiphany, oh ebony passion fruit! One melancholic gaze and slight raising of his ears sends me into a series of $180°$ flips peculiar to my breed.

Tomorrow seems days away.

Dottie's Mission

To rid royal parks of all dogs and + common people. Definition of a CP? Don't know till I have one in my mouth.

DOTTIE'S MISSION:

TO RID PARKS OF ALL DOGS AND COMMON PEOPLE.

DOTTIE'S DEFINITION OF A CP?

DON'T KNOW UNTIL I HAVE ONE IN MOUTH.

As I leap from the back of the car, the cloying smell of a fecund female fills my nostrils. A bitch in season means Melchior will not be concentrating on me.

My enemy, Pharos, stands on the steps, her eyes bulging in triumph. Is it possible that her ancient, arthritic body could manufacture the 'must musk'?

I have hated Pharos since we met. She belongs to my Mummy's Mummy and feels superior. Frolicking with Melchior I disdain her venomous asides.

MY FORMAL PORTRAIT. I FEEL IT CAPTURES MY SENSITIVE
AND CONTEMPLATIVE NATURE. ▶

I felt sorry for her. Just imagine being a corgi, a sort of paraplegic Alsatian.

Melchior's smell, as sweet as a lime tree's blossom, distracts me. He is locked up in the kennels behind the kitchen. He is whining and his amber eyes are wet with unrequited lust.

I press my nose against the chicken wire. I give my finest display of 180° leaps but he just stares in the direction of Pharos who has followed me. I am rejected, vanquished and lie panting against the wire. Melchior contemplates my pink tummy with as much interest as an anorexic for foie gras.

I LIKE TO RELAX SOMETIMES. ▶

Melchior's master approaches. 'Poor Dottie,' he says. His sympathy only adds to my humiliation. He has come to take Melchior for a walk and puts him on a lead. Melchior nearly strangles himself trying to reach Pharos.

This is going to be a terrible Christmas. I wander back to the house. Pharos eyes me with sadistic joy.

I find Mummy. She is talking to her Mummy. They are animated and happy, they must be talking about horses.

I LIKE TO USE MY PMT CONSTRUCTIVELY.

(DEAD SQUIRREL FOR BREAKFAST) ▶

'Hello, Dottie,' says Mummy's Mummy. I try to look cheerful and clear my mind of her association with that moth-eaten sponge of infamy.

'We hope you and your coevals are going to behave,' Mummy's Mummy continues. I sit with one leg splayed like a baboon. My head hangs defensively over my chest as I feel the lecture has only begun.

'Just look at those frightful jaws! We do not know what you see in bull terriers.' At this point Mummy lowers her head, scowls and defiantly sticks her leg out.

I SCENT THE MUST MUSK.

'They look like sharks. How did you become obsessed with this monstrous breed of wart hogs? They are sure to have a taste for blood after they savaged that child in the park. We do not want them here next Christmas.'

If this is going to be my last Christmas, I might as well make it memorable.

THE FECUND FEMALE AND MELCHIOR. ▶

Christmas day. It is cold and we race around the sundial in the garden. The family return from church and we go inside. The Christmas tree is decorated and surrounded with presents.

Pharos and the other corgis position themselves near the tree, anticipating their Christmas stockings. A deep resentment grips me. With every breath my growl grows to a battle cry. Death to the enemy!

I am in flight across the presents, dragging tinsel like a feather boa across my chest.

I THINK CORGIS ARE BEST SLAUGHTERED, HALAL STYLE, AND THEN SERVED
ON A BED OF CHRISTMAS WRAPPING PAPER — CROSS-CULTURE CUISINE!

Mummy screams, 'No, Dottie!' Pharos stares, her smugness turns to horror as the tinsel terror locks jaws.

Cataracts of scarlet rain soak my face and decorate the gaily twinkling baubles. Suddenly there is no more 'must musk', or resistance from Pharos's moth-eaten body. My rage takes away my senses and I am numb to the desperate attempts of the humans to disengage my fangs from Pharos's neck.

Pharos waits for her Christmas stocking. I wait for Pharos.

Various methods are being applied: kicks, screams and much soda water. The scrum of humans, jets of Schweppes and barking bitches help to enmesh me in the shiny twine. The Christmas tree falls. I lie battered but at peace beneath the great conifer. Shattered crystal balls, broken stars and a mangled fairy surround me. I release my grip on Pharos's neck.

The day is mine but the night in the kennels is a long one.

PEOPLE LOVE ME BECAUSE I AM REFERSHINGLY DIRECT. ▶

I had bad dreams about a firing squad.

The consolation prize for being confined to death row is that Melchior is in the cage next door. I have not told him why I am in disgrace.

His master comes in the morning. I notice there is no lead. Perhaps this means that Pharos is no longer on heat. Mummy's oldest brother sadly says, 'Oh, Dottie, you monster, what have you done?'

I recall how lifeless Pharos's body was when I released her to forage for chocolate under the tree. I shift from paw to paw uneasily.

Eglantine and Florence find me. They tell me Mummy's Mummy is in tears and Pharos is dead. There have been terrible threats of execution.

Florence has contributed to our disgrace. A maid was sweeping up the Christmas tree decorations and commented to the butler, 'That Florence looks like an albino Mike Tyson and would you keep him as a pet?' Florence bit her knee.

Apparently we are leaving today.

It was a joyless return home.

Mummy is sad and remote. I try to cheer her up. I chase my tail. Finally Florence and I corner her in the study while she is on the telephone. She is having a serious conversation, what a challenge! Bull terriers hate to be ignored. I tackle her leg with vehement passion whilst Florence barks and jumps on and off the sofa with increasing speed. Mummy puts down the telephone. Her anger turns to helpless laughter.

THE TRIUMFEMINATE.

House arrest is not so bad.

Mummy puts us on a lead when we go out. We pull and rarely agree on the direction proposed by our charioteer. This makes the expedition more interesting, especially for the press who pursue our every move.

I enjoy fame, although I would like more access to my public.

I WOULD LIKE MORE ACCESS TO MY PUBLIC. ▶

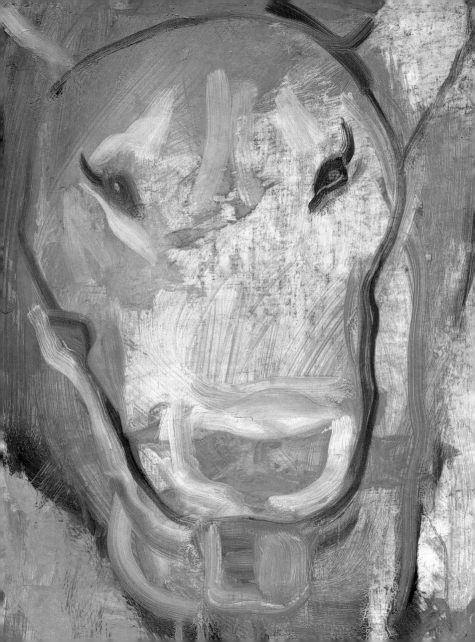